Geek Out!

THE MODERN NERD'S GUIDE TO
COSPLAY

BY KRISTEN RAJCZAK NELSON

Gareth Stevens
PUBLISHING

Please visit our website, www.garethstevens.com. For a free color catalog of all our high-quality books, call toll free 1-800-542-2595 or fax 1-877-542-2596.

Cataloging-in-Publication Data

Names: Rajczak Nelson, Kristen.
Title: The modern nerd's guide to cosplay / Kristen Rajczak Nelson.
Description: New York : Gareth Stevens Publishing, 2018. | Series: Geek out! | Includes index.
Identifiers: ISBN 9781538211977 (pbk.) | ISBN 9781538211991 (library bound) | ISBN 9781538211984 (6 pack)
Subjects: LCSH: Cosplay–Juvenile literature.
Classification: LCC GV1201.8 N45 2018 | DDC 793.93–dc23

First Edition

Published in 2018 by
Gareth Stevens Publishing
111 East 14th Street, Suite 349
New York, NY 10003

Copyright © 2018 Gareth Stevens Publishing

Designer: Sarah Liddell
Editor: Joan Stoltman

Photo credits: Cover, pp. 1, 9 Frozeficent/Wikimedia Commons; texture used throughout StrelaStudio/
Shutterstock.com; pp. 5, 15, 16 Phillip Maguire/Shutterstock.com; p. 6 Sean Pavone/Shutterstock.com;
p. 7 Wanblee~commonswiki/Wikimedia Commons; pp. 11, 20 Shirlaine Forrest/Contributor/WireImage/Getty Images;
p. 13 Nigellegend/Wikimedia Commons; p. 14 Lauren DeCicca/Stringer/Getty Images Entertainment/Getty Images;
p. 17 Dissident93/Wikimedia Commons; p. 19 Niemti/Wikimedia Commons; p. 21 CarlaVanWagoner/
Shutterstock.com; p. 23 petch one/Shutterstock.com; pp. 24, 25 Daniel Boczarski/Contributor/Getty Images
Entertainment/Getty Images; p. 26 AdamBMorgan/Wikimedia Commons; p. 27 Danny Choo/Wikimedia Commons;
p. 29 Albert L. Ortega/Contributor/Getty Images Entertainment/Getty Images.

Printed in the United States of America

CPSIA compliance information: Batch #CW18GS: For further information contact Gareth Stevens, New York, New York at 1-800-542-2595.

CONTENTS

Words in the glossary appear in **bold** type the first time they are used in the text.

A WHOLE NEW WORLD

Imagine your favorite character from a video game, comic, book, movie, or TV show. What do you like about them? Maybe you love the strength of Korra from *The Legend of Korra*. Or maybe you think Captain America is Marvel Comics's best good guy.

If you think you'd like to dress up and act like your favorite character, you should try cosplay! The word "cosplay" is short for "costume play." It's a popular hobby some people have even turned into a career! From creating your own costumes to traveling to **conventions**, there's a part of cosplay for every geek out there.

SOME ASSEMBLY REQUIRED

Sometimes you'll need help with your cosplay! Make sure to ask an adult for help when you're using a glue gun or cutting plastic. If you aren't sure how to make something, an adult may know or be able to help you find it online.

SPIDERMAN, MARVEL
COMICS CHARACTER

People used to use names like "geek"
and "nerd" to make others feel bad. Today, a
"geek" or "nerd" is someone who's **passionate**
about a subject, whether that's cosplay,
collecting, or playing board games!

5

Cosplay conventions as they're known today began in 1940. When Forrest Ackerman and Myrtle R. Douglas went to the World Science Fiction Convention the year before in futuristic costumes, they became the first reported sci-fi convention goers ever to dress up. The next year, so many people dressed up that a costume contest was held! Soon, conventions started having masquerades, or big costume parties!

The term "cosplay" wasn't around until the mid-1980s to describe a convention in Los Angeles, California. While fans in Japan and elsewhere had been dressing up for years, there was finally a perfect English word for it!

Today, cosplay is very popular in Japan.

MORE THAN A CENTURY OF COSPLAY

Though the first cosplay convention may
have been in 1940, this was not the
beginning of cosplay. Cosplay is one
part of a long history of people making
costumes at home for Halloween parties
and masquerade balls! As early as 1908,
people were making and wearing costumes
of their favorite characters from
comic strips.

GETTING STARTED

The first step to cosplay is deciding who or what to be! It's easy to choose someone who looks a little like you. For example, people with brown hair could easily dress up as Frodo from *The Lord of the Rings*. Are you nervous about cosplay? Choose a character who wears a mask or head covering, such as Baymax from *Big Hero 6*.

The most important part of choosing your cosplay is picking a character from something you love. After all, you'll be spending a lot of time creating the costume and acting like the character!

SIMPLE IS GREAT

Are you new to cosplay? It's okay to keep your costume simple! You can wear a Batman T-shirt or choose a character that wears regular clothes, such as Ash from *Pokémon*. Some people like to sew and build costumes, but you don't have to do that to be a part of the wonderful world of cosplay!

Cosplay is a way of showing that you're a fan. If you love *Power Rangers*, why not cosplay as your favorite ranger?

HAIR AND MAKEUP

Now it's time to work on your look! Someone cosplaying as Jack Skellington from *The Nightmare Before Christmas* will need to wear makeup. You might also decide to wear makeup instead of a mask. Getting cosplay makeup to look right takes practice. You can ask someone who has cosplayed before to help. Plus, there are lots of videos and guides to cosplay makeup online.

You'll want to learn how to do your hair like your character, too. Many people simply wear a wig, but wigs can be hot and uncomfortable to wear for a long time.

TRY IT OUT

Before you buy a bunch of makeup, try out products on your hand or arm first. Many people have **allergic reactions** to costume makeup, including red and itchy patches. Many makeup stores let you "try before you buy," but be sure to ask before you open anything in a store!

Jack Skellington doesn't have any hair! To look bald, you can wear a rubber headpiece called a bald cap and add makeup to look like Jack.

MORE THAN PLAYING DRESS UP

One of the biggest parts of cosplay is putting your costume together! Planning is very important. Think about how much time you have. If you need your costume tomorrow, you may not have enough time to make one. That's okay! Buying a costume doesn't mean you won't have fun!

You can get a costume ready in just a few days by using parts of costumes you already have, your clothes, and your toys as **props**. If a character's look focuses on one piece, like an awesome hat, consider having a simple costume and put your time or extra money into making that one piece extra cool!

KEEP IT COMFY

While it would be great to look *exactly* like a character, it's just as important to be comfortable. Think about how long you'll have to wear your costume, what the weather might be like, and more. Don't wear a long-sleeve top made out of fleece if you'll be cosplaying outside in summer!

It doesn't matter if you buy or make your own costume as long as you love being that character!

Many cosplayers take months to make costumes! It takes a lot of practice, patience, and skill to sew and fit a costume. Many **fabric** stores offer sewing and clothes-making classes. It's a long path to making more **elaborate** and special costumes, but everyone has to start at the beginning!

A good way to work on your costume is to figure out what's going to take the longest or be the hardest to make and start there. Most importantly, make sure your costume fits you! Even if it isn't exactly the same as your character's, if it fits you well, you'll look great!

Part of creating your costume is choosing what fabrics to use. Keep in mind when picking fabric that some are very expensive—even ones that may make your costume look perfect!

INCLUDE YOUR GROUP

Cosplay gets even more fun with other people! Ask classmates, neighbors, or family members to dress up as their favorite characters. You can help each other make costumes, do makeup, and make props. Most importantly, you can take lots of great pictures when you're done!

HOMEMADE POWER LOADER
SUIT FROM THE *ALIEN* MOVIES

THE COST OF COSPLAY

When planning your cosplay, think about how much money you can spend. Costumes can cost nothing if you use what you have at home or just a little money if you only buy a couple of pieces. However, something custom-made by a **professional** could cost hundreds of dollars.

Sewing your own costume is just one part of cosplay creation. What if your character has a different costume for battle—and you'd rather make that? Many cosplay costume makers use **materials** other than fabric in their costume designs, such as hard foam and plastic pipes called PVC pipes. Plastic sheets call Worbla can be melted and shaped into just about anything, from fancy helmets and armor to gloves with claws.

Some cosplayers are so committed, they make their own props, too! They may have special skills such as metalworking to make their props **authentic**. Some even sell their creations for others' cosplay!

A prop can make a good costume into a great costume. You might consider saving your money to buy a great prop you can use over and over again.

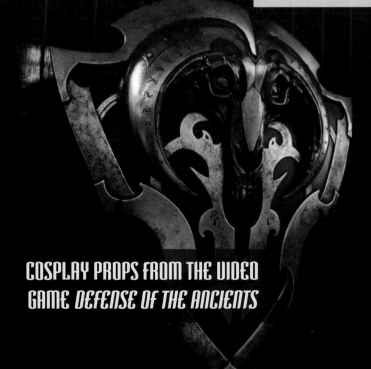

COSPLAY PROPS FROM THE VIDEO GAME *DEFENSE OF THE ANCIENTS*

BE YOUR CHARACTER!

When you put on a costume in cosplay, it's more than just wearing it! You have a chance to try out that character's **persona**. This can be scary if the character isn't a lot like you. But don't let that stop you! Put on your costume, do your hair and makeup, and be proud of expressing your fandom!

Famous cosplayer Jessica Nigri once said of cosplay: "It's the creativity and the freedom to be yourself, but not yourself." Cosplay can help you build **confidence** as you try out different parts of your character's personality in public!

YOUR FAVORITE HOLIDAY!

Halloween is a great time to practice cosplay! You can easily make your favorite character a part of this spooky holiday's fun. Add some zombie makeup to your Alice in Wonderland costume or extra spider webs to a Spiderman costume. Test out new costumes to see if they're ready to wear!

Before Jessica Nigri really got into cosplay, she says she wasn't very sure of herself. But once she started cosplay, she says, "All of a sudden . . . it was like, 'You are awesome,' and . . . instant acceptance."

19

TAKE IT TO A CON

Cosplay has gotten more and more popular around the United States! Comic and sci-fi conventions today include many parts of popular culture. Fans of the Harry Potter series are just as welcome as those who love the classic 1960s issues of *The Fantastic Four*.

Cons are huge opportunities for cosplayers to show off their latest costumes. More than that, it's a place for fans to meet! Cosplay brings people together. Online cosplay communities often meet up at cons across the country. Sometimes they're all dressed as characters from the same movie, video game, or show!

This group all dressed up as characters from *Attack on Titan* at the MCM Comic Con in Manchester, England.

SAN DIEGO COMIC CON

SAN DIEGO COMIC CON

Comic-Con International: San Diego is one of the most famous comic cons in the world. It started in San Diego, California, in 1970. Since nearly the beginning, it's been more than comics though. The event is open to fans of all kinds of popular culture. Today, more than 130,000 people attend—many are cosplayers!

Convention goers don't just do cosplay. They often get to meet the actors or creators of their favorite characters! Cons have talks that give fans chances to learn about new projects or ask questions. Some cons are small, and some are huge, crowded, high-energy events. What kinds of talks and meet-and-greets they offer can be really different.

Do you love *Toy Story* or *Frozen*? Disney theme parks and special events are great places to cosplay, too! Special events for new movies often have lots of cosplay. Sometimes you can even meet the character you're dressed as while at Disney!

PLANES, TRAINS, AND AUTOMOBILES

Many people travel to cons, even taking cross-country flights to go to the biggest ones. That may change what you can bring! Is your **replica** *Zelda* sword allowed on a plane? Do the wings for your costume of Marvel Comics's Dark Angel fit in the car?

FAMOUS US CONS

EMERALD CITY COMIC-CON
SEATTLE, WASHINGTON

CHICAGO COMIC AND ENTERTAINMENT EXPO
CHICAGO, ILLINOIS

NEW YORK COMIC-CON
NEW YORK CITY, NEW YORK

WONDERCON
ANAHEIM, CALIFORNIA

COMIC-CON INTERNATIONAL: SAN DIEGO
SAN DIEGO, CALIFORNIA

MEGACON
ORLANDO, FLORIDA

Check out this map of famous comic and pop culture cons throughout the country. Are any near where you live?

COSPLAY TO WIN

Many cons have cosplay contests. There's often a chance for contestants to win money! Everyone gets to show off the many months of work that went into their costume, whether they win or not. These events generally allow only costumes that are homemade or mostly homemade. Because of that, there might be different awards for **amateur** cosplayers than there are for professionals.

There are even cosplay contest TV shows! *Heroes of Cosplay* followed both new and experienced cosplayers as they imagined, created, and competed in cosplay. On *Cosplay Melee*, four cosplayers face off while creating costumes and characters.

C2E2 CROWN CHAMPIONSHIP COMPETITOR

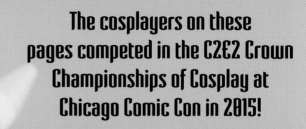

The cosplayers on these pages competed in the C2E2 Crown Championships of Cosplay at Chicago Comic Con in 2015!

MORE THAN LEARNING TO SEW

Some cosplayers work with a team to make a great costume. Someone on their team may even have gone to school to learn fashion design or theater costuming. Since they learned to design, sew, and construct costume pieces from teachers and professionals, they have a great advantage in cosplay!

GO PRO?

Being a professional cosplayer is possible, but doing it as a full-time job isn't very common. That's partly because there's no one way to make enough money to live on doing cosplay alone. Some, like Lindsay Elyse and Jessica Nigri, sell signed photographs of themselves in costume to fans online. They may be hired by companies to go to cons dressed as characters from their games, movies, or comics. Cosplayers may even be paid to fly to cons as far away as Tokyo, Japan, and Paris, France!

In order to get these opportunities, cosplayers first need to gain fans. They often use social media to reach people and get fans!

Anthony Misiano is a well-known cosplayer who commonly dresses as the Joker from the *Batman* comics.

ENAKO, FAMOUS
JAPANESE COSPLAYER

THE SOCIAL IMPACT

Amie Lynn, a part-time professional cosplayer, has more than 83,000 followers on Instagram as "Miss Habit." Nigri has 2.3 million! Social media tells fans where they'll be and what new costumes they're making. Companies can find out who's popular by seeing how many followers they have—and hire them for cosplay!

MAKE IT YOUR OWN

Creativity is a big part of cosplay. Some people work hard to look exactly like the character they're playing, but you can also be creative and change parts of the look to make it your own!

TOP TIPS

- Start simple: If you're new to cosplay, try out a costume made out of things from home before you buy fabrics and try to make a costume from scratch!

- Be comfortable: Make sure you don't mind wearing your costume, hair, and makeup for a long time if you need to.

- Buy key pieces: Need the perfect sword or necklace? There are lots of places and people that sell great pieces for cosplay!

- Have fun: Cosplay is about enjoying your favorite characters, so there's no need to be too serious!

If you want to dress as Princess Amidala from the Star Wars movies, but you're worried about being too warm in her long dress, make your Amidala dress have a shorter skirt! You can be an evil Superman—or even a girl Superman! The world of cosplay accepts everyone, however they'd like to dress! The only rule is that you should be having fun while doing it!

You can even mix two characters into one costume! These cosplayers have combined *Toy Story's* Jessie and Woody with Jedis from the Star Wars movies!

GLOSSARY

allergic reaction: the condition of the body being affected badly by sensitivity to usually harmless things in the surroundings, such as dust, pollen, or makeup

amateur: someone who does something without pay

authentic: made the same way as the original

confidence: belief in oneself

convention: a gathering of people who have a common interest

elaborate: something with many small or fancy parts

fabric: cloth

material: something used to make something, such as a fabric

passionate: having strong feelings

persona: the way someone acts

professional: earning money from an activity that many people do for fun

prop: the object a character carries or uses that makes them recognizable

replica: a copy

FOR MORE INFORMATION

BOOKS

Larson, Jessica, and Karen Larson. *FX! Makeup and Costumes.* Huntington Beach, CA: Teacher Created Materials, 2017.

Mihaly, Christy. *Getting Paid to Make Cosplay Costumes and Props.* New York, NY: Rosen Publishing, 2017.

Wolfe, Brian. *Extreme Costume Makeup: 26 Creepy & Cool Step-by-Step Demos.* Cincinnati, Ohio: Impact Books, 2013.

WEBSITES

Fun and Easy Sewing Projects for Kids
so-sew-easy.com/fun-easy-sewing-projects-kids/
Practice your sewing for future costume making with these simple projects.

20 DIY Superhero Costume Ideas
diyprojects.com/superhero-costume-ideas/
Try out these easy-to-make costume ideas if you'd like to cosplay as a superhero!